WELCOME BACK TO SCHOOL
ACTIVITY BOOK

S C H O L A S T I C
PROFESSIONAL BOOKS

New York • Toronto • London • Auckland • Sydney
Mexico City • New Delhi • Hong Kong • Buenos Aires

Cover design by Maria Lilja
Cover illustrations by Bob Masheris
Interior design by Maria Lilja
Interior illustrations by Bob Masheris, Rick Brown, Rusty Fletcher

ISBN 0-439-18842-3

Contents

Introduction

Welcome back to school! Getting the school year off to a great start is important for both students and teachers. The beginning of the school year is a time for you to learn about students' abilities and interests. It's also a time to initiate routines and set the tone for learning. For students, it is an exciting time to meet new classmates, adjust to an unfamiliar environment, and find out what they can look forward to in the year to come.

Whatever your approach to the first days of school, your goals probably include most, if not all, of the following:

* building a sense of community;

* establishing rules, routines, and other boundaries;

* helping children get to know the classroom space, as well as the other people in the room;

* encouraging children to look forward to learning each day; and

* providing a welcoming and engaging environment.

To help you achieve these goals, this book contains a wonderful variety of learning-filled games, a short play, bulletin board ideas, reproducible activity pages, and more. Turn to this book for tried-and-true classroom-building ideas your students will love.

You'll find activities that help settle down and focus students, as well as those that get them into an enthusiastic, "I can do it" frame of mind. Best of all, each activity in the book requires minimal preparation!

We've also included ideas for getting organized: convenient checklists to help you remember the things you need to do and the supplies you need to get, a sample newsletter to send home to parents, and even tips for preparing for substitute teachers. You'll find ways to get started with class rules and routines, fun listening activities, and lots of other engaging activities that help build community in the classroom.

Make the start of this school year the best yet!

Roll Into Learning

To liven up your classroom instantly, try the Roll Into Learning bulletin board set (Scholastic, 2003). The bright and colorful set is perfect for welcoming your students back to school. It includes 31 ready-to-personalize, kid-pleasing animals on skateboards and skates. A teaching guide provides lots of ideas on using the set for classroom management and displaying children's work, as well as cross-curricular connections for language arts, math, science, and social studies. It's a perfect way to roll into the new school year!

Before the First Day

It's no secret that when you prepare for something, the sooner you start and the more time you devote to it, the easier it will be. The checklists and tips in this section can help you prepare for the first day of school with ease.

Prep-Steps Checklist (page 8)

The Prep-Steps Checklist is intended to help you with all the pre-term preparation you need to remember to do. Copy this list each year to help prepare you for the first day of school.

Save This! Checklist (page 9)

Copy and post this list as a reminder of materials to save for class projects. This list also includes ways to put these materials to work. You may also want to send copies of this list home to parents so they know what you need them to save and donate.

Procedures Checklist (page 10)

Use the categories on this checklist as guidelines to create your own checklist for classroom procedures.

Classroom Organization Checklist (page 11)

This page lists important things to consider when organizing your classroom (including safety reminders).

Class List and All-Purpose Chart (pages 12 and 13)

The reproducible class list and all-purpose chart will come in handy for recording all sorts of things all year long!

Flexible Grouping Techniques (page 14)

This page suggests how (and when) to group students randomly, by ability or skill, for cooperative learning, by interest, task, or knowledge of subject, as well as student choice. You can use this all year long.

Letters Home (page 15)

A weekly newsletter is an effective way to communicate with parents on a regular basis. Try sending the first one out before the first day of school to help students look forward to coming to your class.

Preparing for Substitutes (page 19)

Prior to the first day of school, develop Plan B and Plan C to minimize disruptions to learning.

TIPS!

* Set time limits for tasks.
* Take advantage of the time you spend waiting in line, at an appointment, for meetings to begin, and so on.

Prep-Steps Checklist

CLASSROOM

- ❑ Decide what will go on bulletin boards:
  • Where will you post announcements, the lunch menu, and a calendar? • What kind of welcome-back display will you put up? • Which boards will be for subject-area work? • Where will students' original work be displayed?
- ❑ Set up learning centers
- ❑ Make signs for room
- ❑ Post your name, class, and room number on both the board and the door, where parents and students can easily see them
- ❑ Make class list to post on door
- ❑ _____
- ❑ _____

STUDENT INFORMATION

- ❑ Prepare class rolls and permanent records
- ❑ Prepare packets for students to take home the first day. Include:
  - ❑ Emergency forms
  - ❑ School rules
  - ❑ Supplies
  - ❑ Bus or transportation rules
  - ❑ Notes to parents
- ❑ Check to see which students may be going to special classes
- ❑ Prepare a file for correspondence from parents
- ❑ Make a checklist for returned forms (can be used later for report cards, etc.)
- ❑ _____
- ❑ _____

SUPPLIES

- ❑ Textbooks
- ❑ Supplemental materials
- ❑ Plan book
- ❑ Grade book
- ❑ Attendance materials
- ❑ Paper clips
- ❑ Construction paper
- ❑ Manila folders
- ❑ Adhesive labels
- ❑ Different kinds of tape
- ❑ Rubber bands
- ❑ Stapler and staples
- ❑ Handwriting paper
- ❑ Scrap paper
- ❑ Spare pencils and pens
- ❑ Sticky notes
- ❑ Tissues
- ❑ _____
- ❑ _____

OTHER LOGISTICS

- ❑ Reconnect with other teachers
- ❑ Find out schedules for lunch, gym, art, music, and library
- ❑ Check out Read-Alouds and other library books
- ❑ Set up a substitute folder. Include:
  - ❑ Daily schedule (fill in as soon as possible)
  - ❑ Seating chart (fill in as soon as possible)
  - ❑ Reproducible activities (across content areas)
- ❑ Prepare a file for faculty bulletins
- ❑ Write tentative lesson plans for the coming week
- ❑ Duplicate materials needed for the first few days
- ❑ Find out how to add information to the school's Web site (if available)
- ❑ _____
- ❑ _____
- ❑ _____

Adapted from _Learning to Teach_ by Linda Shalaway (Scholastic, 1998)

Save This! Checklist

SAVE THIS:	TO USE FOR:
❑ **Paper bags**	Costumes, masks, fold-away towns, wigs, puppets, forms for papier-mâché animals
❑ **Plastic lids**	Coasters, frames, mobile parts, molds for plaster plaques
❑ **Buttons**	Jewelry, mosaics, eyes for stuffed animals, collages, games
❑ **Pantyhose/stockings**	Weaving, braiding, knitting, crocheting, soft sculpture, heads for dolls or puppets
❑ **Nuts, cones, pods, and seeds**	Mosaics, jewelry, decorated wreaths, candle rings, boxes, frames, flower pictures
❑ **Stones, shells, and water-smoothed glass**	Paperweights, sculptures, jewelry, mosaics
❑ **Pressed flowers, leaves, and grass**	Place mats, window transparencies, collages
❑ **Rug and tile samples**	Hot-dish mats, covers for small books, mosaics, fuzzy boxes, dioramas
❑ **Odd mittens, gloves, and socks**	Finger and hand puppets, clothes for small dolls
❑ **Hangers**	Simple mobiles, cloth banners, weavings, masks
❑ **Scrap wood**	Toys, carvings, construction, games, building blocks, printing blocks
❑ **Bits of string, yarn, and cord**	Weaving, stitchery, knitting, crocheting, braiding, string painting, animal tails
❑ **Gift wrap paper**	Collages, paper weaving, paper chains, origami, beads, dioramas
❑ **Old jewelry**	New jewelry, accents in ceramics, holiday ornaments, collages
❑ **Wire**	Armatures for papier-mâché or clay sculpture, flexible skeletons for cloth dolls, jewelry
❑ **Plastic meal trays**	Printmaking, necklaces, frames, dioramas
❑ **Plastic packing chips**	Decorative chains, constructions
❑ **Foil pans and trays**	Plaques, ornaments, jewelry, lanterns, rhythm instruments
❑ **Egg cartons**	Containers, sculptures, animals, planters
❑ _____	_____
❑ _____	_____

Adapted from article in _Instructor_ (October 1980) by Diane Crane

Procedures Checklist

Beginning Class

- ❑ Roll call, absentees
- ❑ Tardy students
- ❑ Get-ready routines
- ❑ Distributing materials
- ❑ _____
- ❑ _____

Work Requirements

- ❑ Heading papers
- ❑ Use of pen or pencil
- ❑ Writing on back of paper
- ❑ Neatness, legibility
- ❑ Incomplete work
- ❑ _____
- ❑ _____

Instructional Activities

- ❑ Signals for students' attention
- ❑ Signals for teacher's attention
- ❑ Student talk during seatwork
- ❑ Activities to do when work is done
- ❑ Student movement in and out of small group
- ❑ Bringing materials to group
- ❑ Expected behavior in group
- ❑ Expected behavior of students not in group
- ❑ _____
- ❑ _____

Ending Class

- ❑ Putting away supplies, equipment
- ❑ Cleaning up
- ❑ Dismissing class
- ❑ _____
- ❑ _____

Other Procedures

- ❑ Rules
- ❑ Lunch procedures
- ❑ Student helpers
- ❑ Substitute procedures
- ❑ Borrowing books
- ❑ _____
- ❑ _____

Room/School Areas

- ❑ Shared materials
- ❑ Teacher's desk
- ❑ Student desks
- ❑ Learning centers, stations
- ❑ Playground
- ❑ Lunchroom
- ❑ Water fountain
- ❑ Bathroom
- ❑ Pencil sharpener
- ❑ _____
- ❑ _____

Assignments

- ❑ Communicating homework assignments
- ❑ Turning in assignments
- ❑ Returning assignments
- ❑ Checking assignments in class
- ❑ Students exchanging papers
- ❑ Making up missed work
- ❑ Marking and grading
- ❑ _____
- ❑ _____

Grading Procedures

- ❑ Recording grades
- ❑ Grading criteria
- ❑ Contracting with students for grades
- ❑ Extra credit
- ❑ _____
- ❑ _____

Academic Feedback

- ❑ Rewards and incentives
- ❑ Posting student work
- ❑ Communicating with parents
- ❑ Students' record of grades
- ❑ Written comments on assignments
- ❑ _____
- ❑ _____

Excerpted from a list developed by the Mid-continent Regional Educational Laboratory, 2550 S. Parker Road, Suite 500, Aurora, CO 80014

Classroom Organization Checklist

Seat Arrangement

Using grid paper, pencil in the shapes and spaces of your room and organize groups or rows of desks. Make it simple to change seating arrangements by writing each student's name on a small sticky note and rearranging as necessary. Keep in mind the following suggestions:

❑ Let the physical layout of the classroom reflect your personality and teaching style.

❑ Arrange the room so that you can make eye contact with every student.

❑ Keep high-traffic areas (like the pencil sharpener) free of congestion.

❑ Create special comfort areas for reading and writing.

❑ Make space available for students to store their belongings.

❑ Label classroom materials to help struggling readers and second-language learners.

❑ Post classroom rules and the discipline policy where students and visitors can see them clearly.

❑ Organize the classroom library by categories, such as genre or theme, to facilitate independent book selection.

❑ Revise your layout as necessary.

Special Safety Checklist:

❑ Fasten rugs so no one trips.

❑ Keep window and door exits unobstructed.

❑ Eliminate frayed cords and other electrical dangers (such as extension cords across a pathway).

❑ Display or store breakable items in safe places.

❑ Safely store art and science supplies—especially anything sharp or toxic.

❑ Review various emergency procedures, such as the fire-drill route.

TIPS!

❋ Place needed materials within reach of your work space.

❋ Move your desk from view of the door to discourage colleagues who may be prone to chat.

❋ Do your best, but avoid perfectionism.

Class List

Name									
1.									
2.									
3.									
4.									
5.									
6.									
7.									
8.									
9.									
10.									
11.									
12.									
13.									
14.									
15.									
16.									
17.									
18.									
19.									
20.									
21.									
22.									
23.									
24.									
25.									
26.									
27.									
28.									
29.									
30.									

All-Purpose Chart

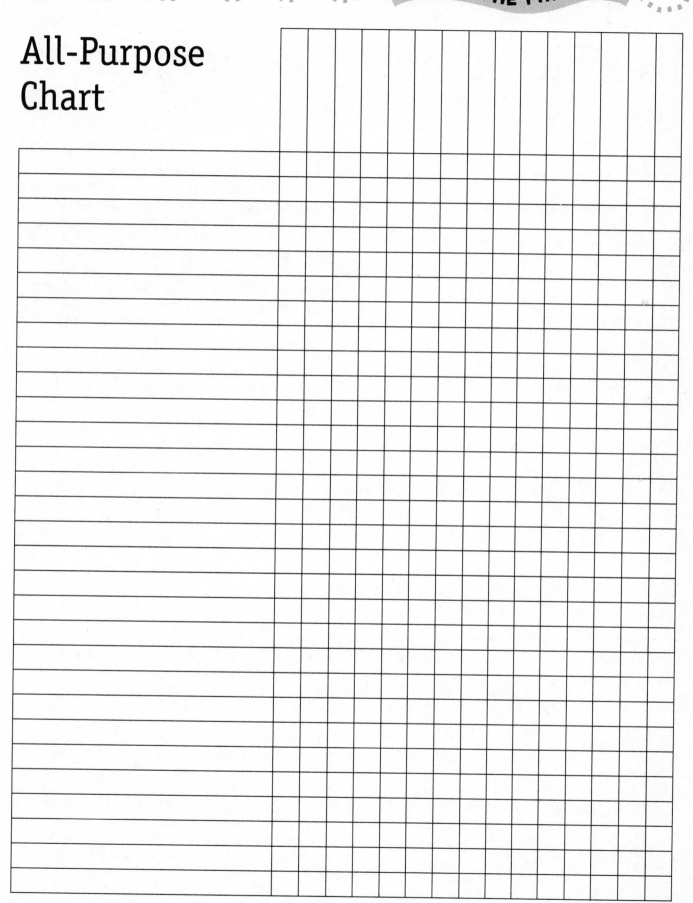

Flexible Grouping Techniques

Grouping Technique	How	Use when . . .	Example
Random	This is completely arbitrary; have students group themselves by like titles or by given colors.	...placement is primarily for management and forming groups of equal size. Also good to use when you are trying to get students to know one another.	Students choose a title from a bag you circulate and group themselves by like title. There are enough titles to form groups of equal size.
Achievement (Ability)	Use performance on a reading measure; students with similar scores are placed in the same group.	...you want to have students read literature selections at their instructional levels as determined by the reading measure.	When completing a folk tale unit, students are directed to read a folk tale that corresponds to their general reading levels.
Social (Cooperative)	Group students according to specific social skills (leaders, followers) heterogeneous in that each has different skills.	...students will need to function in different roles; students learn different roles from one another and work together to complete a group task.	Students read a script and glean important information to share with the rest of the class. When preparing, one person reads, another takes notes, another draws. One child is the group spokesperson.
Interest	This group is based on an interest survey. Assign students to a group or have them assign themselves to a group based on interest in a topic.	...student interest is the main motivating force for learning about a topic.	Students who are interested in a favorite author or illustrator come together to learn more about him/her.
Task	Those who are successful in completing given types of activities are grouped together.	...you want to enable students to use their strongest modality to show understanding.	Children who find drawing enjoyable are grouped together to construct scenery for the reenactment of a story.
Knowledge of Subject	Students with knowledge of a given subject or hobby are grouped together.	...you want students to see likeness among one another and share information.	Students who are interested in baseball cards are grouped together to share the statistics of their favorite players.
Skill/Strategy	Students lacking in a skill or strategy are grouped together.	...you want to teach the skill or strategy to those who need to learn it.	Children who need to learn specific print concepts are grouped to learn them.
Student Choice	Students are allowed to group themselves according to a like characteristic such as author or genre.	...you want to use literature response groups in which students take the lead; also good to use when student success is not dependent on choice.	Several books are displayed and students are invited to choose the book they would like to read. Those with like titles are then put in the same group.

"Flexible Grouping Techniques" adapted from *Flexible Grouping in Reading: Practical Ways to Help All Students Become Better Readers* by Michael Opitz. Copyright © 1998 by Michael Opitz. Used by permission of Scholastic, Inc.

Letters Home

During August, help set the stage for positive attitudes toward school and learning by writing a note to each student on your roster, welcoming the child to your class. Students will look forward to the first day of school, feeling that you are really interested in them. If at any time new students are enrolled in your class, writing a note to them at the end of their first day will help them feel welcome.

Collaborative Classroom Chronicle

A weekly class newsletter is an effective way to foster home–school communication any time of the year. To help both parents and children better know what they can expect in the coming year, try mailing one to each student's family before the school year begins. The newsletter might feature articles on your approach to teaching, the class goals you've set for the coming year, any homework or absence policies, important class rules, the first book the class will read, as well as a list of needed classroom supplies. This is also a good time to mention weekly evaluation, report card, or conference procedures. Here is a sample letter you may want to include in the first newsletter:

Dear Parents,

Please enjoy this first issue of the Classroom Chronicle. I've sent this newsletter home to you to introduce myself, share some of my philosophies on teaching, and give you and your child a hint of what to expect in the coming year. This year promises to be a great one. Your child will be learning many new things this year—academic, organizational, and social skills, as well as self-confidence and responsibility.

In order to keep you informed of your child's progress, I plan to send home a weekly newsletter announcing upcoming projects, reporting on the previous week's activities, and informing you of special needs our class might have. If you have any questions or concerns throughout the year, please do not hesitate to contact me. A note or phone call to request a meeting time in advance will help me to give you and your child my undivided attention.

I am looking forward to meeting you and your child. I'm looking forward to working with you this year as we help your child reach his or her maximum potential and experience all the joys of learning.

Sincerely,

Classroom Chronicle: All Year Long

Creating a classroom newsletter on a regular basis may seem like yet another responsibility. By sharing the task with students, you can provide not only necessary information to parents, but also a quick and easy way to publish students' writing on a regular basis. Monday through Thursday, choose one student each night to write one or two complete paragraphs about something he or she did that day, what was learned from the experience, and how he or she felt about the day's activities. The next day that student will type the information into the computer, including a title, name, and date at the top of the article. By the end of the week, four different students will have written about the school day and added the article to the computer. (If no computers are available, students should neatly rewrite the information onto a sheet of paper.)

At the end of the week, write a brief article that describes your thoughts about the past week, information about upcoming events and thematic units, requests for parent volunteers, and so forth. Add your brief article, as well as the four student articles, to the Classroom Chronicle template (pages 17–18), include some related clip art, copy the newsletter, and send it home to parents. If your school has a digital camera, consider taking snapshots of your students each week to add to the newsletter. Students will connect to their classroom community and practice writing skills. Parents will appreciate being kept well-informed and they will enjoy reading about students' experiences.

CLIP ART

Extra! Extra!
Read All About Us!

Monday

Tuesday

Wednesday

Thursday

Preparing for Substitutes
(and the Unexpected)

So you've made all of your preparations for the first day of school. You're ready to greet your new students and start the school year off right. Out of the blue, an emergency happens. However, an unexpected absence on the first day (or any day) doesn't have to be a disaster, if you're prepared!

Prior to the first day of school, when planning your own classroom procedures (see Procedures Checklist, page 10), pay special attention to how you envision your class having a productive day with a substitute teacher, ensuring that "lost" time becomes "learning" time. You may have already even developed an emergency activity file for this very purpose! It always helps to revisit and add to these ideas from time to time.

The reproducible substitute teacher information form (page 20) is a great way to record all of the essential information a substitute will need. You can use it "as is" or adapt it to suit the particular needs of your classroom. Whatever you use, it is important to familiarize substitutes with daily procedures such as lunch and attendance counts, discipline and other classroom routines, and seating charts. Also, let them know the shortest route to the nearest restroom!

Remember to prepare students as soon as possible for the inevitability of a substitute. As a class, brainstorm possible situations that might lead to a substitute (such as a teacher meeting) or another kind of disruption (such as a fellow classmate getting sick or a parent or the principal knocking on the door). Remind them how they can help the substitute and why their cooperation is important. You can also brainstorm a special version of the class rules. Write them on a chart. Ask students to sign it showing they agree to follow these rules when there is a substitute or another disruption. And if the consequences of breaking the rules are also posted, this can minimize less-than-optimum behavior when you're not around. You might even wish to include behavioral expectations for substitute days in your first newsletter.

One of the most effective ways to find a reliable substitute is to thank those who do a good job in your classroom. You can call or write them a note. Inform the principal when you've had an exceptional substitute and ask for them each time you are in need. The continuity of the same great substitute time after time is ideal.

TIPS!

* Create a form letter to students encouraging their good behavior in your absence.

* While detailed lesson plans will help you feel more at ease, when possible give substitutes the chance to teach. Most can—and want to—undertake genuine teaching responsibilities.

* Create a folder that contains quick warm-ups and ready-to-go work such as the reproducible sheets and short activities found in this book. This limits the paper to go through and provides a place to put collected work. Keep a list of a few books students are sure to love hearing read aloud.

* Ask the substitute to list negative *and* positive experiences of the day. You may want to develop a form or checklist.

Substitute Teacher Information

Where to Find . . .

Class list _____

Seating chart _____

Attendance record _____

School map / Floor plan _____

First-aid kit _____

Lesson plans and materials _____

Supplementary activities _____

Rainy day activities _____

Gym equipment _____

Art supplies _____

Emergency Procedures _____

_____

Classroom Procedures

When students finish early, _____

_____

Students with exemplary behavior may _____

Students who are disruptive may _____

_____

People Who Can Help

Teacher / Room _____

Administrator / Room _____

Dependable students _____

Support Teacher(s)	Time / Location

Special Schedules/Needs

Name	Special Need(s) / Services

Instructional Assistants / Student Teachers

Name	Role	Schedule	Time / Location

The First Day

The first day is the most important one during the first weeks of school. It is crucial to create a positive first impression. Students will view both your actions and the classroom environment as informal cues to your expectations of them. If classroom activities flow smoothly, students will notice and, ideally, behave accordingly. One way to set the tone for a productive year is to have an assignment ready to go on the first day—so students can begin working as soon as class begins.

The Reading Connection (page 22)

To help reduce first-day worries and lighten everyone's mood, try sharing a good story or laugh as a class. Turn to page 23 for a list of some just-right first-day books to read aloud.

Name Games (page 24)

Typically, students answer roll call with a standard "Here." To liven up this procedure—and learn a little about your students—try some alternate ways to take attendance.

Student Information (page 25)

Gathering student information on the first day is a necessary, but often time-consuming, task. A reproducible student information form (page 26) will make gathering student information as easy as possible.

Class Rules and Routines (page 27)

Presenting classroom rules and routines as you would a regular lesson is an effective way to familiarize students with many of the situations they'll encounter over the course of the year. While there are bound to be a few rules not open to discussion, it's helpful to involve students in brainstorming some classroom rules. Share the read-aloud play (page 28) with your class to precede the brainstorming process.

Getting to Know You (page 32)

Discovering similarities among one another is a favorite part of the back-to-school season. Remember to help students "get to know" the important features of the room and the school, as well.

TIPS!

* There's no match for arriving early. Give yourself plenty of time so that your stress level remains in check, and you have time to put your things away and be at the door in time to greet students with a welcoming smile.

* Try starting students with something they already know how to do, such as a simple drawing or writing activity, or a word search. This will help them feel successful and confident.

Listening Activities (page 35)

The opening days of school are such a whirlwind of activity that some of your students may find it hard to concentrate. So here are a few activities to help them do just that.

Reproducible Activities (page 38)

If possible, limit the amount of clerical work you do on the first day. Also try to avoid leaving the room while students are there. However, providing a ready-to-go activity or two for students can keep them productively engaged from the start, allowing you to take care of any necessary details as they arise.

Cursive Nameplate: This is an instant cursive alphabet. Students can practice tracing both upper- and lowercase letters, and write and display their own names.

First-Day Challenge: Students can work on their own or in pairs. For an extra challenge (or in teams), ask them to include more than one answer per box.

What's Wrong With This Picture?: Find ten zany things in a classroom scene: wacky clock, rain under the umbrella, dog-student, fish outside window, upside-down flowers, calendar, girl on swing, girl in pajamas, missing desk leg, flippers for shoes.

Back to School: Find the correct path through the maze to get from home to school.

Hidden Words: This word search contains twenty school-related words.

The Reading Connection

Opening-Day Book Sharing

Promote enthusiasm for reading throughout the year by sharing your love of reading on the very first day of school. Describe your favorite books and ask pupils to tell you about theirs. Encourage them to share what they read during the summer. Was it different from what they read during the school year? Perhaps they read comics, statistics on the back of baseball cards, or directions to a game. Invite children to bring to school and share whatever they enjoyed reading the most.

When children arrive, let them discover books in all sorts of places and containers. Perhaps have books hanging from the ceiling, or piled high in a reading corner. Why not fill a basket with magazines and a toy sink with books? Remember to give children plenty of time to browse through the books.

TIPS!

✳ Remember to write your name on the board so students can learn it immediately. If your name is difficult to pronounce, try dividing it into syllables, or including a phrase like, "rhymes with . . ." You may also invite children to write their own names on the board before sitting down quietly.

✳ Post or store extra assignments in a regular place. Students who finish assignments early will know exactly where to find another one.

Back-to-School Read-Aloud Books

Amber Brown Is Not a Crayon
by Paula Danziger (Putnam, 1994)
What's third-grader Amber Brown
going to do now that her best friend
Justin is moving away?

Amelia's Notebook by Marissa Moss
(Pleasant, 1999)
A nine-year-old records her thoughts
about moving, school, her sister, her
best friend, and a new friend.

Chrysanthemum by Kevin Henkes
(William Morrow, 1996)
Chrysanthemum loves her name—
until she goes to school and the
children make fun of her.

Cloudy With a Chance of Meatballs
by Judi Barrett
(Simon & Schuster, 1982)
Life is delicious in this tall-tale
town where it rains soup and juice,
snows mashed potatoes, and more!

The Giraffe and the Pelly and Me
by Roald Dahl (Penguin Putnam, 1998)
Billy joins the Ladderless Window-
Cleaning Company and gets not only
a new job but also three new friends.

Leo the Late Bloomer by Robert
Kraus (HarperCollins, 1994)
This is the reassuring story of Leo,
a young tiger, who finally blooms—
proving that eventually everyone does.

Lilly's Purple Plastic Purse by Kevin
Henkes (William Morrow, 1996)
When Lilly can't resist showing off her
purple purse, her teacher shares a lesson about apologies and forgiveness.

The Lost and Found by Mark Teague
(Scholastic, 2000)
Two boys show a new girl in school
the Lost and Found, and end up
having quite an adventure.

Measuring Penny by Loreen Leedy
(Henry Holt and Company, 1998)
Lisa learns that there are many ways
to measure a dog.

Miss Nelson Is Missing!
by Harry Allard and James Marshall
(Houghton Mifflin, 1985)
Miss Nelson's class tends to be a little
unruly until substitute teacher Viola
Swamp straightens them out.

The New Kid on the Block by Jack
Prelutsky (Greenwillow, 1990)
Includes over 100 hilarious poems
children will love.

Sometimes I Feel Like a Mouse
by Jeanne Modesitt (Scholastic, 1996)
A child experiences different feelings.

Somewhere Today by Shelley Thomas
(Whitman, 1998)
People bring about peace by caring
for one another and their world.

The Teacher From the Black Lagoon
by Mike Thaler (Scholastic, 1997)
On the first day of school, a boy falls
asleep and dreams that his class is
taught by Mrs. Green—a monster!

Thank You, Mr. Falker by Patricia
Polacco (Putnam, 1998)
Mr. Falker, a very special teacher,
recognizes Trisha's dyslexia
and helps her.

Tom by Tomie dePaola
(Putnam, 1997)
The author draws from his
own childhood in a story
about his grandfather.

We Are Best Friends
by Aliki
(William Morrow, 1991)
This story is about
keeping friends and
making new ones.

*Where Are You Going
Manyoni?*
by Catherine Stock
(William Morrow, 1993)
In Zimbabwe, a child encounters
several wild animals on her long
walk to school.

Some Favorite Authors Born in September

  3   Aliki Brandenberg (1929)

  8   Jack Prelutsky (1940)

 13 Roald Dahl (1916)

 15 Tomie dePaola (1934)

Name Games
Fun Ways to Call Roll and Line Up or Dismiss Students

Attendance

Instead of answering roll call with a standard "Here," during the first week of school, ask children to respond to one of the following questions when they hear their names:

Day 1:   What is your favorite food?

Day 2:   What is your favorite TV show or movie?

Day 3:   What is your favorite holiday?

Day 4:   What is your favorite animal?

Day 5:   What is your favorite game?

The second week of school, you might have students answer these questions at roll call:

Day 6:   In what city or town were you born?

Day 7:   What is your favorite school subject?

Day 8:   When is your birthday?

Day 9:   Who is your favorite celebrity?

Day 10: What color are your eyes?

You are sure to think of many other lively questions to ask students.

Lining Up With a Twist

When you're pressed for time, the quickest way to line your students up for classroom exit is probably row by row or group by group. However, if you've got a few extra minutes, why not try a fun and unusual method? Lining up for lunch or dismissal at the end of the day is a perfect time to play a game using students' names. It requires the use of various language terms and skills. Start by giving a clue about a name. For example: *If your name shares the number of syllables found in "syllable," please line up.* Or: *If your first name contains eight letters, please line up.* If a student (for example, Reynaldo) recognizes the clue as referring to his name, he calls out the name. If correct, that person gets in line. If, in a reasonable amount of time, he does not recognize the clue referring to his name, any student who does may answer though no one may get in line.

TIPS!

* To encourage listening skills, try "quizzing" students on their classmates' responses.

* If several students have similar responses, you may want to use the information for a whole-class graphing activity.

Besides names, you can focus on other student attributes:

1. Students who have green anywhere on their socks, please line up... now students with red on their socks... now students with yellow on their socks ...

2. Students whose favorite ice cream flavor is rocky road... now pistachio... peppermint... banana... strawberry... vanilla... chocolate ...

3. Students whose favorite sport is tennis... soccer... volleyball... swimming... skiing... basketball... football... baseball...

There's no end to the number of clues and categories you can devise for lining up.

Student Information

Gathering student information on the first day is a necessary, but often time-consuming, task. Remember, being as thorough as possible the first time around will help maximize the rest of your classroom time, making it more productive and learning-filled.

Textbook Distribution

To keep track of textbooks, try an alphabetical filing system using index cards. On each card, ask students to list their name, address, and phone number, as well as each subject that has a textbook (you can write a list on the chalkboard or an overhead). Then students can write the name of the textbook and the numbers of each text after the appropriate subject on the index cards. Remind students of your own rules regarding textbooks, such as not marking in them, creating a protective cover for them, whether they are allowed to remove them from the classroom, and what any related consequences are.

TIPS!

* Explain, discuss, and give students a chance to practice such routines as opening-of-day exercises.

* Post a general schedule for lunch, music, physical education, recess, and classwork. Emphasize and teach routines that will help students move into these periods quickly and efficiently.

* Remember, students won't learn classroom routines all in a day. Continue to emphasize and practice for the first few weeks.

Student Information

Name_____

Address_____

_____

Phone number_____

Birth date_____

These are the subjects I like the most (check all that apply):

❑ reading ❑ math ❑ social studies ❑ science ❑ writing ❑ spelling

❑ art ❑ music ❑ gym ❑ other_____

When I don't understand something I usually:

❑ ask the teacher ❑ ask a family member ❑ ask a classmate

❑ try to figure it out on my own ❑ other_____

These are some of the things I can do (check all that apply):

❑ use a computer ❑ play an instrument ❑ take care of a pet ❑ play a sport

To get to school I usually:

❑ walk ❑ ride a bike ❑ take a bus ❑ ride in a car

My favorite kinds of books to read are (check all that apply):

❑ biographies ❑ mysteries ❑ tall tales ❑ historical fiction ❑ nonfiction

❑ adventure ❑ science fiction ❑ other_____

What do you like to do in your free time? _____

_____

Who is someone you admire?_____

_____

What would you like to be when you grow up? _____

_____

What is one of your goals for this school year?_____

_____

Class Rules and Routines

Class Rules and Routines

Presenting the most important classroom rules and routines as you would a regular lesson is an effective way to familiarize students with many of the situations they'll encounter over the course of the year. Once you've explained the routines, open the floor to questions, and give students a chance to practice.

Class-Created Rule List

Ask students to imagine there are no stop signs or traffic lights anywhere on the streets. Why might that be dangerous? Help them to understand that street signs and stoplights keep the streets safer, so that fewer accidents occur.

Then ask: *Why do we need rules in our classroom?* (Some students may not know the answer.) Help them to understand that classroom rules, like street signs, make things safer by telling children what to do.

Present each of the following hypothetical situations. For each one, ask: *What rule could we invent that would make things better?* (Remember never to use the name of a child in your classroom.)

1. Tony threw a baseball in the classroom, and it broke a window.

2. While Ingrid was giving a report, two children were whispering to each other. Ingrid's feelings were hurt.

3. Kevin and Chantal were racing in the hallway. Kevin tripped and skinned his knee.

4. Paolo was talking to a friend while the teacher was explaining the homework. He didn't hear the assignment.

5. Sierra spilled some glue on the worktable and left it there. Later, Calvin put his paper on the table and now the paper is gooey.

On a large sheet of oaktag, write the rules that the students suggest. Challenge students to come up with more situations where rules are needed. Hang the list of rules in the classroom. Chances are it will be strictly adhered to because the students made the rules themselves.

TIP!

Who Need Rules?

Perform this read-aloud play (page 28) early in the school year to help show your new students the importance of following rules. Assign each student a part. The Chorus can be made up of as many students as you wish.

Ask the Narrator, Rule Reciters, and Rule Breakers to read their lines in turn. (Each Rule Reciter should also hold up a sign with the pertinent classroom rule written on it, for example, "Be on time.") The Chorus can recite each classroom lesson—or sing it to the tune of "Twinkle, Twinkle, Little Star."

Who Need Rules?

Narrator

Rule Reciters:
- Rule #1
- Rule #2
- Rule #3
- Rule #4
- Rule #5
- Rule #6
- Rule #7

Rule Breakers:
- Latecomer
- Mr. or Ms. Messy
- Jabbermouth
- Hall-Runner
- Line-Pusher
- Roughhouser
- Bus Show-Off

Chorus

Narrator: Welcome to our classroom play.
It tells of rules we must obey.
You have to follow every rule.
If you don't, you'll be a fool!
Let us see what comes to pass
When rules are broken in our class.

Rule #1: Rule number one: Be on time.
(Holds up a sign that says "Be on time.")

Latecomer: I am Latecomer, late to school.
I thought being late was cool.
But then I missed the work assigned,
And now I've fallen way behind!

Narrator: Latecomer broke an important rule.
What can we learn from this mistake?

Chorus: Be on time to school each day,
You'll know what to do that way.
Class can be a lot of fun
If you're here when the day's begun.
Be on time and don't be late,
Watch the clock and you'll feel great!

Narrator: Now let's see what comes to pass
When another rule is broken in class.

Rule #2: Rule number two: Be neat when you work.
(Holds up a sign that says "Be neat.")

Mr. Messy: I'm Mr. Messy all day long.
I never care what I do wrong.
But once with paint I made a mess
And spilled it on my classmate's dress!

Narrator: Uh, oh! Mr. Messy broke another important
rule. What can we learn from this mistake?

Chorus: When you're working, do be neat,
Don't be messy at your seat.
Careful, careful what you take,
No one wants a spill or break.
Don't be messy, just be neat
When you're working at your seat.

Narrator:	Here's a third rule you should know, If you break it, oh, oh, oh!
Rule #3:	Rule number three: Listen closely when someone is speaking. *(Holds up a sign that says "Listen closely.")*
Jabbermouth:	I'm Jabbermouth, I talk all day, I never hear what people say. But once, on a walk, I got a fright, The class turned left, and I turned right!
Narrator:	Jabbermouth was lost because of not listening to the teacher's directions. What can we learn from this mistake?
Chorus:	Listen closely, listen hard, Always keep your ears on guard. Do not speak when others do, They will think it's rude of you. Listen closely, lend an ear, Never miss what you must hear.
Narrator:	In the hallway, there's a rule You should never break at school.
Rule #4:	Rule number four: Walk in the halls. *(Holds up a sign that says "Walk in the halls.")*
Hall-Runner:	I'm Hall-Runner, on the run, Running in the halls is fun. But one day I ran and tripped, You should see the pants I ripped!
Narrator:	Hall-Runner learned this lesson the hard way. What can we learn from this mistake?
Chorus:	In the hallway, do not run, Falling down is never fun. Walking is the way to go, Not too fast, just nice and slow. Don't go running in the hall, Make the building safe for all.
Narrator:	In the lunchroom line each day, Here's a rule we must obey.

Rule #5: Rule number five: Be patient in the lunchroom line. *(Holds up a sign that says "Be patient in line.")*

Line-Pusher: I'm Line-Pusher, at lunch I love
To cut in line and push and shove.
But one day when I tried to push,
I dropped my lunch, and now it's mush!

Narrator: Line-Pusher went hungry that day.
What can we learn from this mistake?

Chorus: In the lunchroom, do not push,
Or your lunch may turn to mush.
Just be patient, wait in line,
Take your turn and you'll be fine.
Never push, or food may toss,
Apples could be applesauce!

Narrator: On the playground, there's a rule.
If you break it, you're a fool.

Rule #6: Rule number six: Play safely on the playground. *(Holds up sign that says "Play safely.")*

Roughhouser: I'm Roughhouser when I play,
I don't care what others say.
But once I threw Mike in the dirt
And accidentally he got hurt.

Narrator: Roughhouser didn't mean to hurt anyone, but that is what happened. What can we learn from this mistake?

Chorus: On the playground, don't be rough,
Just play safely, never tough.
Have fun when you're in the yard,
Play your best but not too hard.
Cut the roughhouse when you play,
No one will get hurt that way.

Narrator: Our final rule is for all of us
Who come to school on the bus.

Rule #7:	Rule number seven: Stay sitting on the bus. *(Holds up a sign that says "Stay sitting on the bus.")*
Bus Show-Off:	I'm a show-off on the bus, I walk around and make a fuss. But one time, when we made a stop, I fell down and went "KERPLOP!"
Narrator:	After that accident, Bus Show-Off was very sore. What can we learn from this mistake?
Chorus:	On the bus, you must sit down As the driver drives through town. Never stand up in the aisle. You may fall and lose your smile. On the bus, just keep your seat, You'll be safe, which can't be beat!
Narrator:	Those are the rules we must obey In class, at lunch, or when we play. You must follow every rule, If you don't, you'll be a fool. Now let's have a quick review So we'll remember what to do.
Rule #1:	Be on time.
Rule #2:	Be neat.
Rule #3:	Listen closely.
Rule #4:	Walk in the halls.
Rule #5:	Be patient in line.
Rule #6:	Play safely.
Rule #7:	Stay sitting on the bus.
All Students:	We remember all the rules, We will keep them—we're no fools!

Getting to Know You

Get Acquainted Bulletin Board

This activity, which you can begin on the first day of school, can help you become better acquainted with your students by leaving notes for them that they can answer.

First, attach one envelope with each student's name on it to the bulletin board. Then explain to students that every Monday, for instance, you will leave them each a note that they should pick up, read, and reply to.

In the first note, include a little information about yourself. For example, you might write:

> Dear Daniel,
>
> I like to make my own kites and fly them. What things do you like to do?
>
> Your teacher,
> Ms. Manderville

TIP!

On the first day, ask students to bring one special thing from home—a favorite toy, a pillow, a game, a picture. Place all the special things in a quiet corner and let children use it for a reading nook.

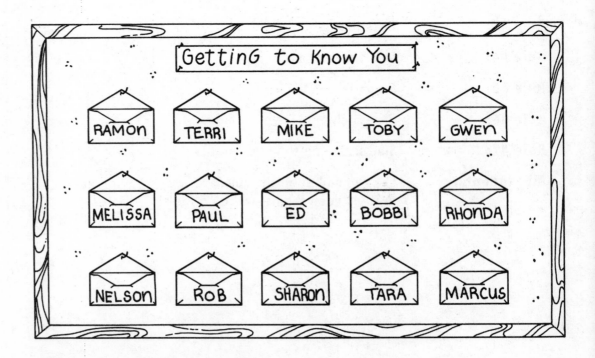

Ask students to write notes in response and leave them in their envelopes for you to find the following day. The second note might tell about an upcoming class activity. For example:

> Dear Sonia,
>
> This week we will make leaf rubbings as a science project. What else would you like to do in class this year?
>
> Your teacher,
> Ms. Manderville

Again, ask students to write notes in response and leave them in their envelopes for you to find the following day.

You might want to read aloud to the class some of the letters you received. Discuss your students' hobbies or the activities they would like to do as a class.

Do You Remember?

This activity can be used to facilitate quiet time, to engage students, and to help you get to know them better.

Write ten questions on the chalkboard or an overhead. (See the following sample questions.) Ask students to try to write answers to all of the questions. When they're done, collect their papers (or journals). You may be surprised what you learn!

Sample questions:

* *What was the last movie you saw?*
* *What was the first sentence you spoke after waking up this morning?*
* *What was the last vegetable you ate?*
* *Where were you last Sunday night at six o'clock?*
* *What is the earliest moment in your life that you can remember?*
* *What was the first book you ever read by yourself?*
* *What was the weather like last Saturday?*
* *What was the first birthday party you ever went to, besides your own?*
* *What was the last holiday you celebrated?*
* *When did you last pet an animal?*

TIP!

Hand out five index cards to each student. Ask them to write one question on each card (about the school, classroom, daily routine, or anything else on their minds).
Sample questions:

1. *What books will we read this year?*
2. *Will we keep the same seats all year?*
3. *Will we go on a field trip?*
4. *When can we go to the bathroom?*
5. *How long is recess?*

Collect all the cards and put them in a box. Pull a card at random and answer the question. Continue the activity as long as it is helpful. For the first week of school, you may wish to spend a few minutes each day answering questions.

Classroom Discoveries

At the beginning of the school year, children often want to investigate all the nooks and crannies of your classroom. Why not turn this discovery period into a game?

Write ten questions on the chalkboard or an overhead. (See the following sample questions.) Challenge each student to find at least one answer to every question. When students are done, have them share their answers with the class. You'll be amazed at the variety of items they discovered.

Sample questions:

* *Can you find something made of wood?*
* *Can you find something made of plastic?*
* *Can you find something made of metal?*
* *Can you find something taller than you?*
* *Can you find something shorter than you?*
* *Can you find something that is green?*
* *Can you find something that has rounded corners?*
* *Can you find something that has wheels?*
* *Can you find something you can see through?*
* *Can you find something that locks?*

TIPS!

* To boost confidence and ease fears, begin the year with simple academic activities that guarantee a high success rate. These can serve as trial runs for practicing such routines as turning in completed work or asking for assistance.

* Have an activity laid out on each child's desk so children can be productively engaged from the start and you can take care of "housekeeping" details. Try something students already know how to do, such as a simple drawing or writing activity, or a word search.

Listening Activities

Observation

Is a picture really worth a thousand words? Show an ordinary photograph to your students and see how many things they can tell you about it. A few questions might be necessary to stimulate their thinking. For example, with a photo similar to the picture at right, you might ask:

* *Is the sun out?*
* *About how many trees can you count?*
* *Is the sun to the right, left, behind, or in front of the photographer?*
* *Is the photographer facing north?*
* *Is it sunrise or is it sunset?*
* *Are there trees to the left of the photographer that are not pictured? How can you tell?*

Tell Me About It

A variation on the Observation activity above is Tell Me About It. Show your class a large intricate picture, either from a Big Book, a poster, or a projection that you shine on the wall. Allow the class to study the picture for one full minute. Then remove the picture and see how many details each student can recall.

Ask questions such as:

* *How many people were in the picture?*
* *What color was the woman's dress?*
* *What was the boy carrying in his right hand?*
* *What animals were in the picture?*
* *How many people wore hats?*

Children love this type of activity, so even if you forget to do it often, your class will remember to ask for it!

Anybody Listening?

Try whispering. Improve students' listening skills with a new twist on the old game Simon Says. Instead of speaking the commands in a normal voice, whisper them. This is also a great way to slow down the pace of a game while capturing the children's attention.

Write your full name in cursive.

Name_____   Date_____

First-Day Challenge

Fill in each of the boxes below. Each word you write must
begin with one of the letters in *First Day*.

	Food	TV show or movie	Famous person	Clothing	City, state, province, or country
F					
I					
R					
S					
T					
D					
A					
Y					

Name _____   Date _____

What's Wrong With This Picture?

Find and circle ten things that are wrong in this picture.

Back to School

Find the correct path from home to school.

SCHOOL

Name _____ Date _____

Back to School Word Search

Can you find all of these hidden words in the puzzle? Circle each one.

bell   chair   desk   glue   office   principal   stapler
bus   chalk   eraser   library   paper   ruler   teacher
cafeteria   clock   field trip   notebook   pencil   scissors

C	H	A	R	L	K	I	E	T	R	I	P	A	E	R
A	L	I	U	A	I	S	Z	A	E	S	E	Q	R	M
F	I	E	L	D	T	R	I	P	R	I	N	C	A	E
E	B	O	E	D	E	P	B	L	U	C	C	N	Y	L
T	S	U	R	K	J	A	M	E	G	H	I	H	S	A
E	S	B	A	P	E	P	A	R	L	A	L	S	E	O
R	P	U	G	L	U	E	W	A	C	L	O	T	K	R
I	L	R	S	J	A	R	D	E	S	K	C	A	I	S
A	A	O	I	C	L	O	C	K	F	X	I	P	E	C
N	U	F	A	N	O	T	E	B	O	O	K	L	J	I
L	G	F	T	E	C	A	T	E	A	C	H	E	R	S
Q	U	I	W	C	H	I	E	R	A	S	E	R	G	S
G	M	C	H	Q	A	F	P	D	B	I	O	B	L	O
U	L	E	N	O	I	L	F	A	I	T	L	H	U	R
L	I	B	R	A	R	Y	K	C	L	Z	O	I	K	S

First Week & Beyond

You've gotten through the first day of school successfully and any jitters and nervousness have subsided. Now it's time to refocus and continue building on your first-day momentum. Before you know it the classroom community will be in full swing.

Following Directions (page 44)

Practice with following directions is a great way to start any day. Students will look forward to it if you give it a fun twist. Any directions given orally reinforce listening skills.

Community Building (page 45)

One of the first steps toward community building is for students to learn their classmates' names. Another important step is for students to learn which of their classmates' names go with which faces. Once students know their classmates' names and can put names to faces, it's time to start finding out what they all have in common. These activities make getting to know one another's names, faces, and interests fun!

Reproducible Activities (page 49)

Scavenger Hunts and Classmate Interview:

These are great ways for students to discover interesting facts about their classmates (or the school). Distribute one of the question sheets (pages 49–52) to each child. Give students 15 minutes (more or less if you desire) to answer the questions by circulating among classmates and briefly interviewing each other. Only one answer is needed for each blank.

TIPS!

* Be fast, firm, fair, and predictable in enforcing rules.

* Reinforce good behavior by commenting on it.

All About Me Flip Book: Students create flip books that tell about themselves.

Materials

- double-sided copies of the All About Me template (pages 53 and 54)
- scissors
- stapler
- colored pencils

1. Copy the templates for the flip book back-to-back as they appear in the book. Give one template to each student.

2. Have students cut out the three panels along the thick solid separating lines.

3. Direct students to fold each panel along the dotted line as shown above.

4. Help students slip the panels together so they can see the titles for each panel. Fasten the top of each book with two staples.

5. Students should follow the directions on each of the panels to complete their flip books.

Super Categories: First decide if you or your students will select the letters to use in Super Categories. Then copy and distribute one sheet to each student or student pair. You can determine the number of words they should come up with.

Who Am I? Glyph: Copy and distribute one sheet to each student. Students should use the legend on the page to decorate the faces so they represent themselves. For a quick bulletin board, ask students to cut out their pictures on the dotted line. Then label a bulletin board, "Meet Room XX" and post all of the pictures.

Picture Writing Prompts: Copy and distribute one sheet to each student. (You can also copy, cut out, and laminate each prompt to use in a writing center.) Ask students to read their stories aloud to show that different people can see the same thing different ways.

Writing Prompts: Copy and distribute one sheet to each student. (You can also copy, cut out, and laminate each prompt to use in a writing center.) Ask students to simply make a list of things in a category. You can also ask them to use the prompt to help them write a story.

Wacky Words: Copy and distribute the Wacky Word puzzle sheet: newspaper column, the light at the end of the tunnel, school crossing, jump in the lake, lost in the woods, around in circles, break all the rules, little sister, new underwear.

Home–School Connection (page 60)

School Stationery: Use this reproducible sheet for notes to students. You can blank out the writing lines to use it for notes to parents. You can also copy it for students to use in a letter-writing activity.

While You Were Out: This handy form can be used to let students know what work they missed due to absence, and when it's due.

Reward Coupon: Use this reward coupon as an incentive for both academic and behavioral achievement.

Weekly Evaluation and Conference Reminder: Keep parents apprised of their child's progress and encourage conferences, as necessary. Remember to invite parents in to hear good news, as well!

Parent Volunteers and Thank You!: Parents' help is an invaluable resource. Don't hesitate to request it. Follow up with a thank-you note to encourage additional help.

Ask Me About...: Help parents to focus their children when asking them about their day at school. You can list the things you'd like students and parents to discuss. As the year goes on, suggest that children come up with their own topics about the school day.

Days to Remember in September

* **Labor Day** (First Monday)
* **Grandparents Day** (First Sunday after Labor Day)
* **Citizenship Day** (17)
* **International Day of Peace** (21)
* **Autumnal Equinox** (22 or 23)
* **American Indian Day** (Fourth Friday)
* *Constitution Week*
* *Hispanic Heritage Month*
* *Library Card Sign-Up Month*

Following Directions

Preposition Practice

Here's a following-directions starter to try that reinforces positional words. Whisper a direction for each child to follow upon entering the classroom:

* *Put your hand **on** your head.*
* *Put your hand **under** your chin.*
* *Put your hand **behind** your ear.*
* *Put your hand **over** your head.*

Ask children to keep their hands in place until they reach their seats.

Wild Walk-Ins

Try this follow-directions activity that also builds vocabulary in action words. As each child arrives, whisper a verb that describes how to enter the room (you may need to demonstrate). For example: hop, skip, jump, walk, stroll, jog, glide, stride, and tiptoe. You may also ask kids to describe to you how they would like to enter the room (subject to your approval).

Picture Grids

First trace a simple picture onto graph paper. Next give each student a sheet of blank graph paper (page 65). Each child begins at a common starting point and follows a set of directions you give orally. Then describe which lines to draw to complete the picture. Directions may be given in terms of left, right; up, down; or north, south, east, west. By counting squares and following the lines on the graph paper, students find outlines of pictures forming on the graph paper. The pictures may be filled in as imagination indicates. As children learn the meaning of the term *diagonal* or such directions as northeast, southwest, and so on, diagonal lines may be added to the picture.

TIPS!

* Write each student's name on a wooden stick and place the sticks in a can. Draw names from the can randomly as a fair way to call on students.

* Have a participating student choose the next person to participate. For gender equity, a boy must choose a girl. A girl must choose a boy.

* To select fairly between two students or groups who want to volunteer, vary the use of tried-and-true methods. Try:
  • rock-paper-scissors,
  • flipping a coin,
  • drawing straws,
  • rolling a die for the highest number, or
  • guessing a number you have secretly recorded.

Community Building

Learning Names

Class List Spelling Bee

This special spelling bee is designed to help students remember their classmates' names. The procedure is simple:

Have everyone stand up. Then select a student and give her the first name of a classmate to spell. If she spells it correctly, give her another name to spell, and so on. If a student misspells a name, ask her to sit down, and choose another student to spell it.

If you run out of first names, use students' last names (or even middle names, if necessary). The winner of the spelling bee is the last student left standing in the room.

Word Search Puzzle

Students will love hunting for their names in a custom-made word search puzzle.

On a piece of plain paper (or graph paper), create a puzzle that contains each of your students' first names. The names can run horizontally, vertically, and diagonally. Make copies and distribute one to each child. Then see who is first to circle all of the names. If it's very early in the year, you might want to provide students with a list of class members.

Linking-Name Game

This activity challenges students to link the letters of their names to those of their classmates.

Write the first names of all students on the chalkboard or on a sheet of paper that you duplicate and hand out. Give each child a piece of graph paper, making sure the boxes are big enough for students to write letters inside.

Challenge students to connect as many names as possible. The names can be connected either horizontally or vertically. See if anyone can link three, four, or more names together. Can anyone link the entire class?

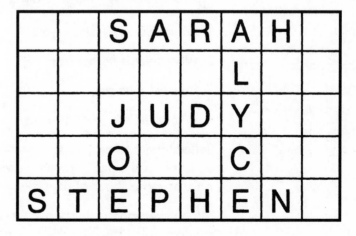

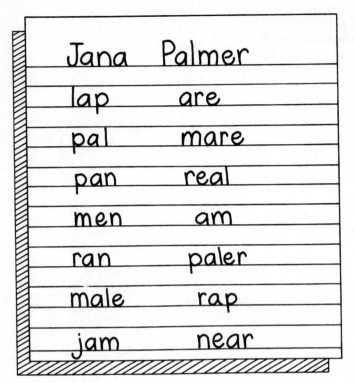

Jana Palmer

lap	are
pal	mare
pan	real
men	am
ran	paler
male	rap
jam	near

What's in a Name? Game

Ask students this riddle: *What belongs to you, but other people use it more than you do?* The answer: *Your name!* This activity lets students use their classmates' names in a creative exercise.

Ask each student to write his first and last name at the top of a piece of paper. Collect the papers and redistribute them at random. (If anyone gets his own paper back, have him switch with someone else.)

Challenge students to create as many words as they can from the letters in the name at the top of the page. You can set a time limit such as five minutes, or allow children to take it home overnight.

When the activity is complete, have each student read the name he received and the words he made from the letters of that name.

Learning Faces

Guess Who? Game

This writing exercise is a fun game and effective way for students to get acquainted with their new classmates.

Begin by having each student write his name at the top of a piece of paper. Collect the papers and redistribute them at random. If a child receives his own name, ask him to trade papers with a neighbor.

Since students may not know everybody's name, have each child stand up and introduce himself. Then write questions on the board, such as:

1. *What color are his/her eyes?*

2. *What color is his/her hair?*

3. *How tall is he/she?*

4. *What is he/she wearing today?*

Tell students to answer the questions about the child whose name appears on the paper they received. Have them write their responses on that same sheet of paper.

When everyone is finished, collect the papers and choose one at random. Read the description aloud. How many classmates can guess who the subject is? Continue reading the papers aloud until every child has been described.

Mystery Photo Game

It's easy to identify a person from his photo, but not so easy when only a fraction of that photo is revealed, as in this fun-filled activity.

Take a photo of each child in your class. Have your students gather in a group close to you. Secretly select one photo and place it in an envelope. Very slowly, start to pull the picture from the envelope. Stop when the top of the subject's head is visible. Then ask: *Can anyone identify this person?*

If no one can guess correctly, pull a little more of the picture out of the envelope. See which student can be the first to identify the classmate. Repeat the activity using several or all of the photos.

For another challenge, you can show just the eyes, nose, or mouth of a photo.

More Fun With Mystery Photos: Baby Pictures

For a fun twist on the Mystery Photo game, ask students to bring in baby pictures (you may even choose to join in this game). Post the pictures in random order and ask students to guess which of their classmates is in which baby picture!

Classmate Concentration

This game will also help students match their classmates' names to their faces. Cut pieces of paper so they are the same size as a typical photo. (If a photo is smaller than an average one, you can affix the photo to one of the pieces of paper). Then write each student's name on a piece of paper. If possible, laminate the photos and the name pieces for greater durability.

To play, place all pieces face down. As in a regular memory game, one by one, students should turn over two cards, trying to make a match. This time, the match should be a name to a face. Whoever ends up with the most matches wins!

Getting-to-Know-You Interest Inventories

Scavenger Hunts

This is a wonderful icebreaker any time during the first week of school. It's critical to stick to your predetemined time limit for this activity because with the excitement this activity generates, it will be tempting to let it continue.

Ask students to raise their hands if they have all 15 questions answered. If no one raises a hand, keep going (14, 13, 12) until you can collect a paper with the most completed answers. Review the sheet with the class. Talk to each of the students whose name is listed under each category. Verify that they fit the given category. If they do not, deduct one point from the total. Continue until a winner is established.

Variations:

* Have students work in pairs or small groups.
* Allow students to work on the scavenger hunt during the first week of school.
* Encourage students to find a different classmate for each answer.
* Invite students to make up their own scavenger hunts.

Classmate Interviews

This icebreaker allows students to get to know each other better. Each student gets a chance to be both a star reporter and a sought-after celebrity. When you collect and read the papers, you will learn a lot about each of your students.

Distribute copies of the classmate interview form to each student. Divide students into pairs. For this activity, 20 minutes works best. Give each student 10 minutes to interview their partner, switching roles after the first 10 minutes so they each get a chance to ask and answer questions.

As a class, create a graph that will help students see that they have many things in common. After you have read these papers, you may wish to add them to a classroom time capsule so students can see how their interests have changed, or not, over the course of the school year.

Scavenger Hunt: Classmates Part I

Find a classmate who fits each of the following categories. Record each name
on the lines provided. Try not to use the same person more than twice.
When you have finished, circle each category that also applies to you.

1. **Who has a birthday in September?** _____

2. **Who has green eyes?** _____

3. **Who walks to school every day?** _____

4. **Who lives within two blocks of school?** _____

5. **Who does not have a middle name?** _____

6. **Who is new in the school this year?** _____

7. **Who went to camp this summer?** _____

8. **Who knows how to bake a cake?** _____

9. **Who has ridden a horse?** _____

10. **Whose favorite color is purple?** _____

11. **Whose first name starts with *M*?** _____

12. **Whose family has a blue car?** _____

13. **Who is left-handed?** _____

14. **Who can play the piano?** _____

15. **Who has more brothers than sisters?** _____

Scavenger Hunt: Classmates Part II

Find a classmate who fits each of the following categories. Record each name and follow-up answer on the lines provided. Try not to use the same person more than twice. When you have finished, circle the number of each category that also applies to you.

1. **Loves to read.**

   Name:_____

   Favorite book:_____

2. **Has a younger brother.**

   Name:_____

   Brother's name:_____

3. **Has two older sisters.**

   Name:_____

   Sisters' names:_____

4. **Has tried asparagus.**

   Name:_____

   Likes it?_____

5. **Speaks a foreign language.**

   Name:_____

   What language?_____

6. **Can play a musical instrument.**

   Name:_____

   What instrument?_____

7. **Has a birthday in January.**

   Name:_____

   What date?_____

8. **Plays on a sports team.**

   Name:_____

   What sport?_____

9. **Owns more than two pets.**

   Name:_____

   What are they?_____

10. **Has lived in another state.**

    Name:_____

    Which state?_____

11. **Has two favorite school subjects.**

    Name:_____

    Favorite subjects:_____

12. **Has a magazine subscription.**

    Name:_____

    What magazine?_____

13. **Likes ice cream.**

    Name:_____

    Favorite flavor:_____

14. **Has been to a zoo.**

    Name:_____

    Favorite animal:_____

Scavenger Hunt: School

To learn more about your school, find an answer to each of the following categories.
Record each answer on the lines provided.

1. **What is the mailing address of the school?**_____

_____

2. **When was the school built?**_____

3. **What is the highest room number in the school?**_____

4. **How many windows are in the library?**_____

5. **How many days can you keep a book that you've checked out of the library?**_____

6. **What else can you find in the library besides books?**_____

7. **What vegetables are being served in the cafeteria this week?**_____

_____

8. **How many tables are in the cafeteria?**_____

9. **How many trees are on the school grounds?**_____

10. **How many drinking fountains are at the school?**_____

11. **How many elevators are in the school?**_____

12. **What can you find that is painted blue?**_____

13. **What teacher has been at the school the longest?**_____

14. **What teacher's last name starts with a letter closest**

to the end of the alphabet?_____

15. **How many exit signs can you find?**_____

Name_____   Date_____

Classmate Interview

Take turns interviewing and being interviewed by your partner.
You may be surprised with the things you have in common.

Name of person interviewed: _____

1. If you could be anything in the world when you grow up, what would you be? Why?_____
_____

2. What are your hobbies?_____

3. What kinds of activities do you like to do with friends?_____
_____

4. What kinds of activities do you like to do by yourself?_____
_____

5. What is your favorite sport to watch?_____

6. What is your favorite sport to play?_____

7. What is your favorite book of all time?_____

8. If you could be any animal, which one would you choose? Why?_____
_____

9. If you could be like any one great person, whom would you choose? Why?_____
_____

10. If you were given $1,000, what would you do with it?_____
_____

What else would you like to know about your partner? Think of one last question to ask.

Question:_____

Answer: _____

_____

_____

_____

The Best Book I Ever Read!

Title: _____

Author: _____

I give this book _____ stars.

☆ ☆ ☆ ☆ ☆

My favorite song is _____

My favorite TV show is _____

My favorite food is _____

My favorite drink is _____

My five favorite friends are _____

_____

*On the back, create a mini time line. List one event important to you for each year of your life.

My Favorite Things

I was born on _____

I am _____ years old.

I am in _____ grade.

The nickname I'd choose for myself is

_____

My hero is _____

What characteristics does it take to be a hero?
(check all that apply)

○ Brave   ○ Kind
○ Honest   ○ Smart
○ Curious   ○ Loyal
○ Famous   ○ Friendly

Why does your hero inspire you?

_____

Would you like to be someone's hero someday?

○ Yes   ○ Maybe   ○ No

Meet My Hero

The Biggest Day of My Life

My favorite school activity is ___

My favorite thing to do on the weekend is ___

My favorite sport is ___

My favorite game is ___

FOLD

My mini review:
___

Write a story about the biggest day (or most important event) in your life. Be sure to include who, what, where, when, why, and how.
___

FOLD

My family members are ___

When I grow up I want to be ___

0 1 2 3 4 5 6 7 8 9 10

ALL ABOUT ME

FOLD

Name _____   Date _____

Super Categories

Select a letter of the alphabet for column 2. Then list as many entries as possible in column 3 that match the description in column 1, and that begin with the letter in column 2.

CATEGORY	LETTER	WORDS
a musical instrument		
a bird		
a wild animal		
a type of transportation		
something you slice		
something you wear		
something you read		
a precious gem		
a type of leader or ruler		
an industry		
a body of water		
a city in Europe		
a green vegetable		
a container		
an animal that lives in water		

Who Am I?

Using the legend below, decorate the face to represent you.

HAIR

Brown: I walk to school.

Black: I ride in a car to school.

Yellow: I ride in a bus to school.

Red: I ride a bicycle to school.

EYES

Black: I have a brother.

Brown: I have a sister.

Blue: I have at least one brother and one sister.

Green: I'm an only child.

Add eyelashes if you have a brother or a sister that goes to this school.

NOSE

Triangle: My favorite season is fall.

Circle: My favorite season is winter.

Square: My favorite season is spring.

Diamond: My favorite season is summer.

MOUTH

Smile: I like green apples the best.

Squiggle: I like red apples the best.

Straight line: I don't like apples.

FRECKLES

One for each year of your age

SHIRT

Polka dots: girl

Stripes: boy

CAP

Purple cap: I like reading the most.

Orange cap: I like math the most.

Green cap: I like science the most.

Blue cap: I like social studies the most.

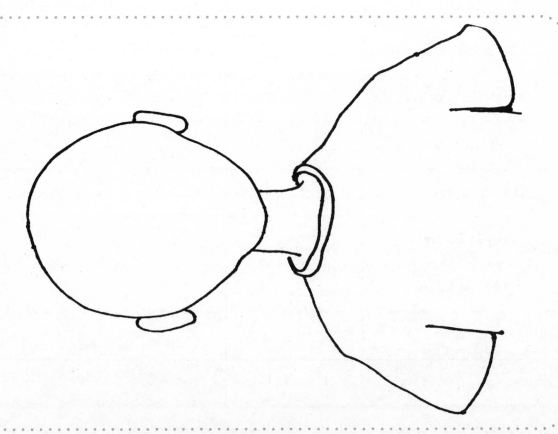

Picture Writing Prompts

Writing Prompts

the sounds in a department store	twilight colors
things that are lighter than a watch spring	things that crumple in your hands
all sounds heard for the next five minutes	things that you love
"squashy" things	things that harmonize
things that hurt	things that reflect
things made more beautiful by age	things found in two's
sour things	happy things
wet things	morning things
things that sparkle under an evening sky	beautiful things
things that chill	adjectives describing people you admire

Wacky Words

These wacky word puzzles represent everyday expressions or familiar words.
To solve them, remember to look at the way the word is placed. Is it up, down, to the right,
to the left, or in the center of the box? Is it over, under, before, or after another word? Does it
remind you of anything? Let your mind play with the ideas. And most important—have fun!

Newspaper	**tunnel** the light	S C H SCHOOL O O L
the jump *lake*	woods LOST woods woods woods woods woods woods woods woods woods woods woods woods woods woods woods woods	around around around
all the rULEs	SISTER	wear new

WHILE YOU WERE OUT

Date:_____

We missed you today, _____.

The homework/classwork that you missed while you were gone is . . .

Math: _____

Reading: _____

Science: _____

Social Studies: _____

Language Arts: _____

Spelling: _____

Other: _____

Your work is due on: _____

REWARD COUPON

Date:_____

Congratulations!

Name:_____

Because of your hard work and cooperation, you've earned a reward!

Reward:_____

_____

_____

Sincerely,

_____
Your Teacher

WEEKLY EVALUATION

Name: _____ **Date:** _____

Homework/Classwork missed for the week:

_____

_____

_____

(All missed work due on Monday, or the next day of school.)

Behavior for the week: ☐ Satisfactory ☐ Unsatisfactory

Comments and Test Grades:

_____

_____

_____

Parent Signature: _____

CONFERENCE REMINDER

Date: _____

Dear _____,

_____

_____

_____

_____

Sincerely,

_____

Your Child's Teacher

PARENT VOLUNTEERS

Child: _____

Dear Parents,

Throughout the year I like to supplement my teaching with guest speakers who are knowledgeable in areas of the curriculum we are studying. I also rely on parent volunteers to help chaperone field trips and aid in classroom activities. Please complete this form and return it to me as soon as possible. Thanks for your help in making this a fulfilling and exciting school year.

Sincerely, _____

Parent(s): _____ Phone: _____

Address: _____

Occupation(s): _____ Hobbies: _____

Other areas of expertise: _____

I would be happy to:
- ❏ Help with classroom activities
- ❏ Supply classroom materials
- ❏ Go on field trips
- ❏ Make phone calls
- ❏ Be a guest speaker
- ❏ Other_____

Comments: _____
_____

THANK YOU!

Date:_____

Dear _____,

_____

_____

_____

_____

Sincerely,

_____
Your Child's Teacher

Ask Me About...